Booker T. Washington

A Buddy Book
by
Randy T. Gosda

ABDO
Publishing Company

VISIT US AT

www.abdopub.com

Published by Buddy Books, an imprint of ABDO Publishing Company, 4940 Viking Drive, Suite 622, Edina, Minnesota 55435. Copyright © 2002 by Abdo Consulting Group, Inc. International copyrights reserved in all countries. No part of this book may be reproduced in any form without written permission from the publisher.

Printed in the United States.

Edited by: Christy DeVillier
Contributing Editors: Matt Ray, Michael P. Goecke
Image Research: Deborah Coldiron, Susan Will
Graphic Design: Jane Halbert
Cover Photograph: North Wind Picture Archives
Interior Photographs/Illustrations: North Wind Picture Archives, Library of Congress, Deborah Coldiron

Library of Congress Cataloging-in-Publication Data

Gosda, Randy T., 1959-
    Booker T. Washington / Randy T. Gosda.
        p. cm. — (First biographies. Set II)
    Includes index.
    Summary: A biography of one-time slave, known for his commitment to education and his role in establishing Tuskegee Institute.
    ISBN 1-57765-734-9
    1. Washington, Booker T., 1856-1915—Juvenile literature. 2. African Americans—Biography—Juvenile literature. 3. Educators—United States—Biography—Juvenile literature. [1. Washington, Booker T., 1856-1915. 2. Educators. 3. African Americans—Biography.]

E185.97.W4 G67 2002
370'.92—dc21
[B]
                                                                    2001034931

Table Of Contents

Who Is Booker T. Washington?

Booker T. Washington is a famous African American leader. Booker was a great teacher, too. Many schools were named after Booker T. Washington.

Booker T. Washington

Booker's First Home

Booker's birthplace.

Booker T. Washington was born in Hales Ford, Virginia. Booker was born in 1856. This was before the Civil War in America.

Booker and his family were slaves. A white man owned Booker's family. Booker's owner was James Burroughs. Booker worked and lived on Mr. Burroughs's farm, or plantation.

Mr. Burrough's plantation was once here.

Booker's mother cooked for Mr. Burroughs. Her name was Jane. Booker had one brother, John. Booker had one sister, Amanda. Booker did not know his father.

Booker and his famly lived in a small cabin. This cabin did not have a real door. It did not have glass windows. There were no beds in Booker's cabin. Booker's family slept on a dirt floor.

Inside Booker's first home.

Growing Up

Booker had different jobs. He carried water to workers in the fields. Booker kept flies away from Mr. Burroughs's dinner table. Young Booker never had time to play. Slaves worked all day long.

An old schoolhouse.

Booker carried schoolbooks for Mr. Burroughs's daughter. He walked to school with her. Booker wanted to go to school, too. He wanted to learn how to read and write. But slaves could not go to school.

Freedom

In 1865, a man came to Mr. Burroughs's plantation. This man read the Emancipation Proclamation. This man said that Booker and his family were free. They were not slaves anymore. Booker's family was happy to hear this great news.

The Emancipation Proclamation

President Abraham Lincoln wrote the Emancipation Proclamation. This important paper freed many slaves. Slavery and the Civil War ended in 1865.

Booker's family left Mr. Burroughs's plantation. They moved to Malden, West Virginia. Booker moved in with his stepfather.

Booker had no time to play in Malden, either. Young Booker worked in the salt mines. He was only nine years old. Booker woke up at 4:00 each morning. He did not get home until after dark.

Mining salt is hard work.

Going To School

Booker's family was very poor. They needed Booker to work. So, Booker did not go to school very much. But he studied at night. He taught himself the alphabet. Booker quickly learned to read and write.

At age 16, Booker heard about the Hampton Normal and Agricultural Institute. This school was for African Americans like Booker. Booker wanted to go to this school. But the Hampton Institute was in Hampton, Virginia. Booker would have to travel about 500 miles (805 km) to get there.

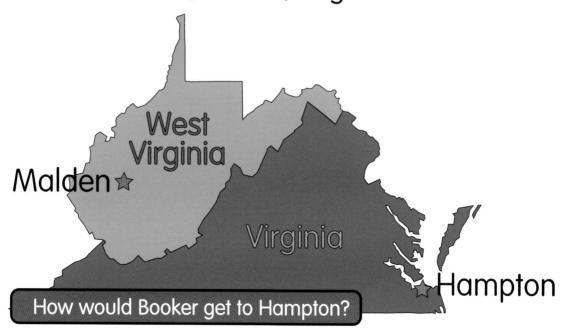

West Virginia

Malden ☆

Virginia

☆ Hampton

How would Booker get to Hampton?

Booker did not have enough money to move to Hampton. But he did not let that stop him. Booker got on a stagecoach. He traveled until he ran out of money. He walked many miles. He slept outside by himself. Booker was tired but happy when he reached Hampton.

People traveled by stagecoach before cars.

Students at Hampton Institute.

Booker loved school. He was a great student. Booker went to class in the daytime. At night, Booker cleaned the school. Booker's job paid for his room and meals.

Booker left the Hampton Institute in 1875. In 1879, Booker became a teacher at the Hampton Institute.

Tuskegee Institute

When Booker was 25 years old, he became the principal of a new school. This new school was the Tuskegee Institute. The Tuskegee Institute was in Tuskegee, Alabama. The Tuskegee Institute was a school for African Americans.

The students of the Tuskegee Institute learned many skills. They learned how to make shoes. They learned how to build houses. They learned how to farm land. The students hoped these skills would help them find jobs.

A class of students at Tuskegee Institute.

Students of Tuskegee Institute built Armstrong Hall.

People from around the country went to Booker's school. The Tuskegee Institute was too small for so many students. So, Booker and his students built a new schoolhouse.

Thanks to Booker, the Tuskegee Institute became famous. President William McKinley visited the Tuskegee Institute. George Washington Carver was a teacher there. George Washington Carver is a famous scientist.

George Washington Carver in his lab.

Booker's Fame

Booker was a good speaker. Many newspapers wrote about Booker's speeches. Booker spoke about schools and jobs for African Americans. People started giving money to the Tuskegee Institute.

President Theodore Roosevelt heard about Booker. He invited Booker to dinner. Booker was the first African American dinner guest at the White House. Booker talked to the president about ways to help African Americans.

The White House is where the U.S. president lives.

In 1900, Booker started the National Negro Business League (NNBL). The NNBL helped African Americans become company owners.

In 1901, Booker wrote a book about his life. This book is *Up from Slavery*.

People today read *Up From Slavery* to learn about Booker T. Washington.

Booker T. Washington is the first African American to be on a U.S. postage stamp.

Booker T. Washington believed in hard work. He worked hard to help himself and other African Americans.

America lost a great leader when Booker died on November 13, 1915. Americans will never forget Booker T. Washington's hard work.

Important Dates

1856 Booker T. Washington is born.

1865 The U.S. ends slavery. Booker and his family move to Malden, West Virginia.

1872 Booker enters the Hampton Institute.

1881 Booker becomes principal of the Tuskegee Institute.

1900 Booker starts the National Negro Business League.

1901 President Roosevelt invites Booker to the White House for dinner.

1901 Booker writes his famous book, *Up From Slavery*.

November 13, 1915 Booker T. Washington dies.

Important Words

African American an American whose early family members came from Africa.

Civil War the United States war between the Southern states and the Northern states. The North fought the South to end slavery.

Emancipation Proclamation President Lincoln freed many slaves with this important paper.

principal the leader of a school.

salt mine a place where people dig for salt.

slave a person who can be bought and sold. Many slaves in the United States were African American.

stagecoach a carriage or buggy pulled by horses.

Web Sites

Booker T. Washington National Monument Home Page
www.nps.gov/bowa/home.htm
This site features Booker T. Washington's life story and information on James Burroughs's tobacco plantation.

Legends of Tuskegee
www.cr.nps.gov/csd/exhibits/tuskegee/intro.htm
This web site highlights the achievements of Booker T. Washington, George Washington Carver, and the Tuskegee Airmen.

Index